THE
W RLD

I
AM
W MAN

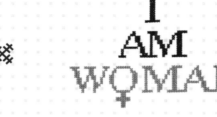

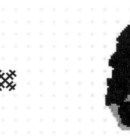

riot grrrl

WOMEN WHO ROCK CROSS-STITCH

By Anna Fleiss and Lauren Mancuso

RUNNING PRESS
PHILADELPHIA

Running Press
Hachette Book Group
1290 Avenue of the Americas, New York, NY 10104
www.runningpress.com
@Running_Press

Printed in China

First Edition: October 2018

Published by Running Press, an imprint of Perseus Books, LLC, a subsidiary of Hachette Book Group, Inc. The Running Press name and logo is a trademark of the Hachette Book Group.

The Hachette Speakers Bureau provides a wide range of authors for speaking events. To find out more, go to www.hachettespeakersbureau.com or call (866) 376-6591.

The publisher is not responsible for websites (or their content) that are not owned by the publisher.

Patterns by Anna Fleiss
Biographical text by Lauren Mancuso
Stitching by Anna Fleiss, Alex Acosta, Sarah Mozal, Athena Ciara-Marenghi,
Lisa Frye, Leah Folta, Jordan Henry, and Rachel Lynn
Photographs by: Steve Legato
Print book cover and interior design by Amanda Richmond

Library of Congress Control Number: 2018947858

ISBNs: 978-0-7624-9178-0 (hardcover)

RRD-S

10 9 8 7 6 5 4 3 2 1

CONTENTS

INTRODUCTION

Women are the original punks. If punk rock is—as its godmother, Patti Smith, once defined it—"the freedom to create, freedom to be successful, freedom to not be successful, freedom to be who you are," then this book features cross-stitch patterns inspired by music's biggest punks from the 1930s to the present day. In an industry long dominated by the mantra that *This is a man's world*, these legendary ladies of rock, hip-hop, pop, R&B, and country kept it real. While women are still rarities at the top of "best of" music lists and classic rock countdowns, the undeniable influence of these female artists, songwriters, and producers has been critical in shaping the sounds of the past and encouraging young girls across generations to pick up an instrument or microphone. Here we pay some long overdue R-E-S-P-E-C-T to women who did more than just rock. This collection of cross-stitch embroidery patterns depicts 20 iconic rockers, soul sisters, and pop phenoms who changed the game, as well as 10 classic song titles to empower musicians and music lovers alike. While they made music at different times and in different formats, these women defined and redefined entire genres, tore down musical and cultural walls, and influenced each other along the way.

Long before Chuck Berry picked up an electric guitar and invented rock 'n' roll, the often-forgotten Sister Rosetta Tharpe was shredding on hers like no one else. As a songwriter, Carole King is responsible for crafting most of the soundtrack of the 1960s, from the number-one girl group hit "Will You Still Love Me Tomorrow" for the Shirelles to the 1967 Aretha Franklin hit "(You Make Me Feel) Like A Natural Woman." Aretha's expressive voice brought soul music to the masses, while Janis Joplin's showed women like Stevie Nicks—who opened for her early on—that they could one day be rock stars, too.

And they weren't the only ones. Patti Smith

helped inspire punk in the 1970s when she set her charged poetry to simple chords; Blondie was the first artist to have a number-one hit featuring rap vocals with 1981's "Rapture"; and Selena transcended cultural boundaries with her unique blend of Spanish- and English-sung songs in the 1990s. Having grown up in poverty, Dolly Parton stands as one of the most prolific songwriters of all time, with hits spanning six consecutive decades. The country queen and multi-instrumentalist also protected the publishing rights to her work from early in her career, ensuring that she would receive proper credit when artists like Whitney Houston took "I Will Always Love You" up the *Billboard* charts a second time.

These badass women were musical innovators in the face of serious obstacles. With her left hand damaged by polio, folk genius Joni Mitchell invented a new way of playing chords while teaching herself the guitar. When her male musician friends warned her against putting too much emotion on display in her lyrics, she did not listen and went on to make 1971's classic album *Blue*. After breaking out as a solo artist in the 1990s, Lauryn Hill faced patriarchal pressure from the music world to ditch her dreams of motherhood in favor of her music career. She refused to listen, writing about her life on 1998's *The Miseducation of Lauryn Hill* and taking listeners on a different but equally honest journey through the female experience.

Then there is renaissance rap woman Missy Elliott, who turned down restrictive record deals early in her career to continue doing it all—performing, producing, arranging, and writing songs for herself and other artists. She maintained complete creative control, and her distinctive sound and music videos shaped hip-hop culture from the 1990s through today. Like Missy, when pop chameleon Lady Gaga faced resistance early on in her career for not fitting the typical mold, she did not listen and continued to do things her own way. As a result, the pop world is a more interesting and inclusive place.

Each of these lady punks—the rock stars, soul legends, gypsy women, independent ladies, and hip-hop visionaries—changed music history by forging their own path and refusing to listen to the noise about how they're supposed to sing, play, look, or be. The women celebrated in this book are not the only talented females to break ground in their respective genres, and they won't be the last.

CROSS-STITCH BASICS

What Is Cross-Stitch?

Before getting started, there are some things you should know about cross-stitch. The first is that cross-stitch is a particular style of embroidery, one in which you'll use a relatively dull needle—called a tapestry needle—to sew x-shaped stitches onto your fabric surface, creating a picture (in our case, of powerful ladies and song titles). Like other kinds of embroidery, cross-stitch can be done on a wide variety of fabrics, including clothes and linens (using a tool called a waste cloth). In this book, though, we'll be working with a particular type of fabric, called Aida cloth, which is designed for cross-stitch.

What You Need

One of the benefits of cross-stitch is how easy it is to get started—you'll only need cross-stitch fabric, tapestry needles, embroidery floss, a hoop, and some sharp scissors, to whip up portraits of your favorite female rock stars in no time.

Let's dig a little deeper into these tools.

FABRIC

Aida cloth is made specifically for cross-stitch projects. It is composed of tiny squares so it is easy to see where each stitch belongs. Aida can be found at your local craft store or online. Pick up a bunch, as cross-stitch can get addictive!

One thing to note about Aida cloth: each piece of cloth will have what's called a "count," also known as the number of squares per inch of fabric. For all of the patterns in this book, you'll want to use 14-count material—this has relatively few squares per inch, and is a good choice for newbies. If you'd like to try more of a challenge, feel free to use a higher count (like 18-count); just know that the higher the count, the smaller your overall design will be once you're done.

To figure out the size of your pattern when you work in a different count of Aida cloth, simply divide the total number of stitches in your pattern (width) by the cloth's count (i.e., a pattern that is 66 stitches across on 14 cloth count is 4.74 inches wide).

NEEDLES AND THREAD

For any kind of embroidery project, you'll need a needle to pull your thread through the fabric. With cross-stitch, the best tool is a tapestry needle—the dull point on these needles will not snag or tear your fabric. Look for size 24 needles when you're gathering your supplies, and consider buying more than you think you'll need.

Thread is the most important, and the most fun, part of your cross-stitch arsenal. All of the patterns in this book use embroidery floss, which is a type of six-strand thread that is especially well-suited to cross-stitch. Each of the patterns will call for thread colors, noted by a DMC number; DMC is the most common brand of floss, and it offers a wide variety of shades. Once you've gotten the hang of cross-stitch, try switching out any of the pattern colors for your own favorite shades.

THE HARDWARE

When you're working on a cross-stitch project, the easiest way to keep your fabric steady is to use an embroidery hoop. These hoops can be made of wood or plastic, and they come in a range of sizes—pick the size that works best for your particular craft (most patterns in this book will need at minimum a six-inch hoop). Your hoop can be removed once you're done with your project, or you can finish you fabric right on the hoop and use it for display.

The more you cross-stitch, the more you'll learn that a pair of small scissors is your best friend. A pair of regular scissors will do in a pinch, but an extra-sharp pair will come in handy if you need to get into small areas or alter your work. Always be careful when using your embroidery scissors—you want to turn that sharpness on your fabric, not yourself.

How to Do It

It's almost time to begin stitching! Cross-stitch is a very straightforward style of embroidery, since it's based around a single easy stitch that you repeat throughout the pattern. And using Aida cloth makes the process even simpler—the squares that comprise the cloth line up with where all of your stitches will be made.

Each of your stitches will be made up of two short strokes, called a top stitch and a bottom stitch. These stitches will cross diagonally, to create an *x* that fills the cloth square. In the patterns, you'll see these stitches noted by a solid square (with a color that corresponds to the thread you should be using). You'll occasionally see lines crossing on top of the patterns; these are called backstitches, and you'll use them to add some details to your patterns. We'll also use satin stitches to fill in the eyebrows in our patterns.

Before you begin stitching your musical masterpiece, you'll need to get your fabric ready. To make sure you have enough room, plan on a piece of cloth that can accommodate your pattern, as well as a healthy border (usually a few inches on all sides). It's better to have a little too much fabric—which you can cut away later—than too little.

The last step is to thread your needle. Find the color that corresponds to the stitches that are in the center of your pattern (more on that in a moment), and get yourself a thread that is between one and two feet long and divide it into strands. Each piece of embroidery floss is made up of six distinct strands, though you will only want to use three at a time when you're stitching. Typically, cross-stitch patterns use only two strands of floss. We'll be using three strands to achieve a denser, more saturated look.

STITCHING

First, find the center of your fabric—you don't need to be super precise, but try to get as close to the center as possible. This is where you'll want to begin stitching. Try folding your cloth in half both horizontally and vertically to find the center.

Your stitches will move from the center of the pattern outward. The patterns in this book use a method called "counted cross-stitch," meaning that you will base your stitches on a pattern, rather than a design printed on the fabric. With this type of pattern, you'll count the number of stitches in the color you're using and then make those stitches on your fabric.

MAKING SINGLE CROSS-STITCHES

1. Once you've found the center of your fabric, you can begin making stitches. To start, you'll want to pull your thread up through the small hole at the bottom left corner of your starting square, being sure to leave a one-inch "tail" of floss on the underside of the fabric. Hold on to that tail as you make your next few stitches—you'll want the back side of your stitches to cover the tail, securing it in place instead of a lumpy knot.

2. Pull the rest of your thread up through the fabric and then sew through the top right corner of the same square, creating a diagonal stitch. You'll want to pull your thread through to the back of the fabric, taking care not to sew it too tightly—your goal should be a smooth surface, without any puckering from the floss. This is the first half of your stitch.

3. To create the second half of your stitch, sew up from the back of the fabric—through the bottom right corner of the square—to the front.

4. Pull your thread relatively taut, and then cross the square diagonally, sewing down through the top left hole. This will create the x shape of your cross-stitch.

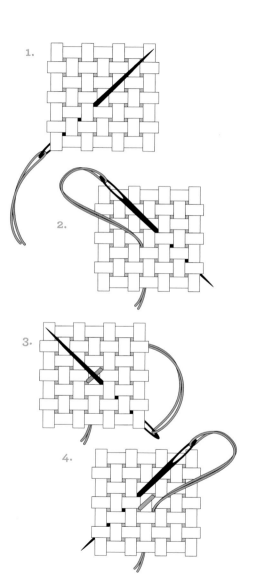

5. Continue by making a stitch in the square next to your completed stitch. This square borders your first stitch, and shares two holes with it.

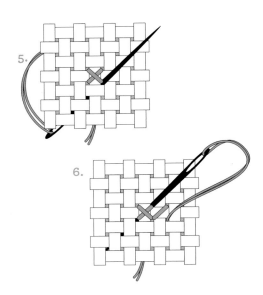

6. The stitches in each square should be made in the same direction, to keep your finished piece nice and even. Your first stitch will again be made from the bottom left to the top right; and then the bottom right to the top left.

MAKING MULTIPLE CROSS-STITCHES

Most of the time, you'll be creating rows of stitches in the same color, not just one isolated stitch. When you're looking to produce big blocks of color, you can use a handy shortcut to create horizontal rows.

1. You'll begin the same way you would for a single stitch—pull your needle up through the bottom left corner of your first square, and stitch across to the top right corner. Instead of finishing off that stitch, begin another half-stitch in the next square, again moving from the bottom left corner to the top right. Repeat this method until you've gone the full width of the section you're working on.

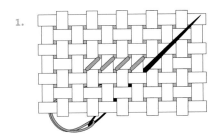

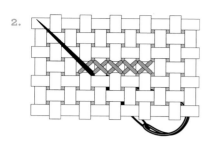

2. Complete each of the half-stitches you just created by moving in the opposite direction, stitching from the bottom right corner to the top left corner of each square. Once you complete the row you're working on, move on to the next row and repeat the method until your color block is completed.

3. When your thread becomes too short to work with easily, simply slip your needle—on the back side of the fabric—under a few stitches (three or four should be fine), pull the floss through, and cut the thread. You'll want to avoid knotting your thread, because that would create bumps that would be visible in your finished piece.

CARRYING THREAD

Most of the time, you'll want to finish a particular color, using the method above, before moving on to a new section. Occasionally, though, you'll want to continue to another section of the same color that is quite close to the one you've just completed. This is called "carrying" the floss, and as long as the sections are no more than four squares apart, it works just fine. Any distance greater than that, and you'll be able to see the floss through the front side of your fabric (especially if you're working on white Aida cloth).

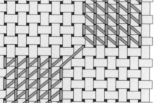

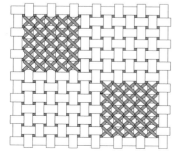

BACKSTITCH

The backstitch is a good friend to turn to when you want to make lines, or add detail to your patterns. To start the backstitch, thread your needle and make two knots in your floss, right on top of each other, leaving a half inch "tail" of floss at the end. Then, find the area where you want your detail line to begin, and, just before that point, push your needle up through the back of the fabric (we'll call this point 1). Your needle should now be on the front side of your fabric. Insert the needle back into the fabric, at the spot where your line should begin (we'll call this point 2). This is your first stitch. To make your next stitch, push your needle up through the back once more, a little ways beyond point 1 (we'll call this point 3). To complete this stitch, come back down through the fabric to close up the gap (we'll call this point 4, though you'll see it's really in the same spot as our original point 1). If you continue with this stitching, you'll keep pushing your needle up through the back of the fabric, a small distance away from the end of your line, and up through the front again to close the line.

In the coming patterns, backstitch is used for all line detail, as well as to outline eyebrows.

SATIN STITCH

Satin stitch is typically an embroidery technique, but in the coming patterns, we'll be using it to fill in the eyebrows of our frontwomen. You'll want to begin by outlining the eyebrows using the backstitch technique you just learned (see left). Then, to fill in the brows, you'll employ the satin stitch.

Start at one end of the eyebrow and push your needle up through the back of the fabric—just inside your outline—and into the fabric just below the top of the outline. Then, push the needle up through the back of the fabric at the bottom of the outline—next to the previous stitch—and back through the top of the outline. Repeat the process until the eyebrows are completely filled in.

Note: For both backstitch and satin stitch, you do not need to go through the pre-set holes in the Aida cloth. In fact, it's more important to ensure that you're precise with your lines, in order to create the details you want in the finished piece. You may even want to use embroidery needles for these stitches, as you may find that tapestry needles are too dull.

PATTERNS:
THE WOMEN

SISTER ROSETTA THARPE

◇◇◇◇◇◇◇ (1915–1973) ◇◇◇◇◇◇◇

GUITARIST, INNOVATOR, PIONEER

Rock 'n' roll was created by a queer black woman in the 1940s. Long before Elvis Presley shook his controversial hips and Chuck Berry strummed his electric guitar, Sister Rosetta Tharpe was howling with feeling while shredding on hers. The forgotten founder of rock 'n' roll brought gospel into nightclubs and concert halls, introduced white audiences to black music, and defied just about every norm there was. As fellow gospel singer Inez Andrews once described her, "She was the only lady I know that would pick a guitar and the men would stand back."

Born in Arkansas, she was billed as a "singing and guitar-playing miracle" at six years old while traveling in an evangelical troupe with her mother across the South. The two moved to Chicago in the 1920s and became fixtures on the city's gospel scene. Rosetta blended urban blues with traditional folk to form her signature style of picking. New York City was her next destination, following a short-lived marriage to a preacher, one of many relationships she'd have in her life with both men and women.

Rosetta became the first gospel performer with a record deal in 1938. Her earliest single, "Rock Me," mixed her growling voice and rockin' guitar with traditional gospel. In New York, she performed shows with famous blues and jazz musicians at Carnegie Hall as well as the Cotton Club and the Apollo Theater, all-white venues at the time. While her reinterpretation of spiritual songs for popular audiences made churchgoing purists shake their heads, her unconventional performances brought gospel music to a wider audience.

Recording for American troops overseas during World War II, Rosetta's popularity grew throughout the 1940s. The 1945 hit "Strange Things Happening Every Day" was the first gospel song to become an R&B hit. With its electric guitar solo and timely lyrics, the song is viewed by some as the first rock 'n' roll recording. Shortly afterward, Rosetta paired up with piano-playing gospel singer Marie Knight to record "Up Above My Head." The two women, who became lovers, often toured together without other musicians, being the only band that they ever needed. Around the same time, Rosetta also played to mixed crowds with the Jordanaires, an all-white male gospel group. Touring the South, her skin tone often prevented her from sleeping and eating in the same establishments as her opening act.

Rosetta's fame peaked in the early 1950s. Her third wedding, which took place at a baseball stadium in Washington, D.C., and the concert that followed were attended by over 20,000. The gig was later released on a record.

At a 1964 performance at an abandoned train station in rainy England, the 49-year-old shredded one more time as the next generation of British blues rockers looked on. While the face of American rock 'n' roll and British blues looks a lot different than Rosetta's, her influence on both genres is undeniable.

	DMC 310
	DMC BLANC
	DMC 3772
	DMC 938
	DMC 3857
	DMC ECRUT
	DMC 976
	DMC 975
	DMC E3821
	DMC 3782

TINA TURNER

◇◇◇◇◇ (1939–) ◇◇◇◇◇

VOCALIST,
QUEEN OF ROCK 'N' ROLL,
POWERHOUSE

With her growling voice and long legs, Tina Turner was a force to be reckoned with. Onstage, she was electrifying. Her explosive way of singing and shaking showed the world that women could rock, too. In contrast to the delicate girl groups of the 1960s, Tina proved that women could also perform songs "nice and rough"—the way she did "Proud Mary." Offstage, Tina was just as tough.

A survivor, Tina received early lessons in perseverance. Born Anna Mae Bullock in Nutbush, Tennessee, she was abandoned by her mother at age 10 and her father at age 13. After her grandmother died, the 16-year-old moved to St. Louis to be with her mother. There, she bumped into Ike Turner, the lead singer of the Kings of Rhythm, at a nightclub. Soon after their meeting, she was singing with the band and often stealing the show. When another singer didn't show up for a recording session in 1960, she sang on "A Fool in Love" instead. Ike renamed her "Tina Turner" for the song's release. He also trademarked the name to keep her from running away with it.

Tina's energy onstage left concertgoers in a trance. In 1966 the pair was approached by Phil Spector, creator of the famous Wall of Sound, to record an album, though he was only really interested in producing Tina. As the story goes, Spector paid Ike $20,000 to record Tina on her own. The superhuman vocals that came out of Tina on "River Deep, Mountain High" remain legendary, even though the song was not a commercial success. She once described the experience to *Rolling Stone*, "I must have sung that 500,000 times. I was drenched with sweat. I had to take my shirt off and stand there in my bra to sing."

Tina kept on rockin' from there. She taught Mick Jagger his moves while the pair toured with the Rolling Stones, wrote the hit "Nutbush City Limits," and became the Who's Acid Queen in the 1975 movie *Tommy*. In 1976, Tina would officially leave Ike, escaping on a bus in the middle of the night with a few cents in her pocket after being roughed up. However, the unstoppable Tina soon found her way back to the top.

With bigger hair and higher heels, Tina became a worldwide success in the 1980s with hits like "What's Love Got to Do with It" and the 1985 release of *Private Dancer*. The album led to three Grammys and a new start for a mid-40s Tina, as sexy and confident as ever. More hits followed, including "The Best" and "We Don't Need Another Hero (Thunderdome)" from *Mad Max Beyond Thunderdome*, in which she also starred. Not only did Tina Turner still have it, she had only gotten stronger.

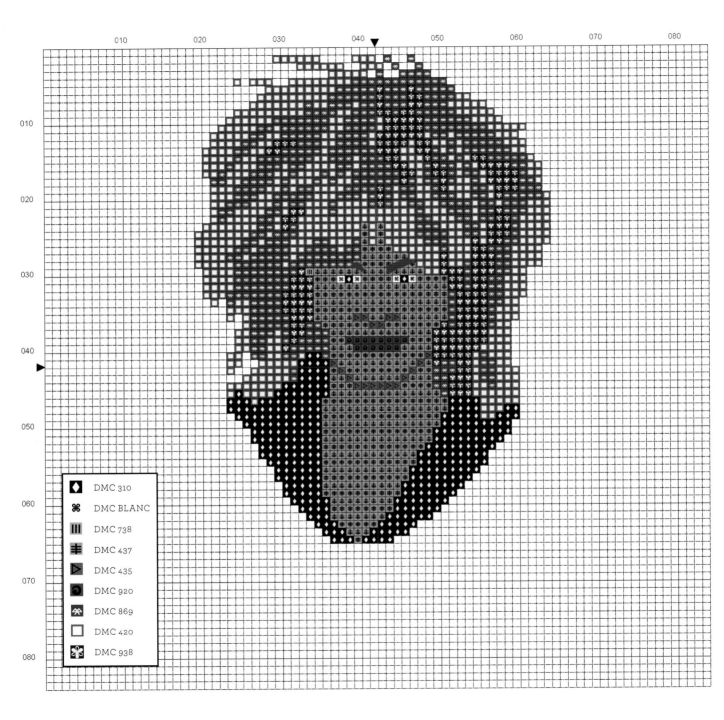

DMC 310
DMC BLANC
DMC 738
DMC 437
DMC 435
DMC 920
DMC 869
DMC 420
DMC 938

Tina Turner

ARETHA FRANKLIN

◇◇◇◇◇◇ (1942–) ◇◇◇◇◇◇

QUEEN OF SOUL, FORERUNNER BIG THINKER

In 1967, a bejeweled crown was placed atop a 25-year-old Aretha Franklin at Chicago's Regal Theater, proclaiming her the Queen of Soul. The coronation came a few months after the release of *I Never Loved a Man the Way I Loved You*. The masterpiece included the enduring anthem "Respect." The hits continued throughout '67 and into '68 with "Baby I Love You," "(You Make Me Feel Like) A Natural Woman," "Chain of Fools," and "Think." Single by single, Aretha transformed music in the late '60s by giving black women a voice as her expressive brand of soul played on radios across America.

The foundations of Aretha's sound, which blended gospel, jazz, R&B, and rock 'n' roll, were in place early. As Aretha was growing up in Detroit, her father, C. L. Franklin, was a famous preacher who was friends with key figures of the civil rights movement and blues and jazz musicians. Naturally talented, Aretha sang and played piano alongside him as a young child and a teenager. Her first recordings were in her father's church at 14, and when he took his sermons on tour across America, the teenager went with him. On the road, she befriended a number of music pioneers, from gospel great Mahalia Jackson to Mr. Soul, Sam Cooke.

Aretha found success on the R&B and pop charts after being signed to Columbia in 1960, but it wouldn't be until her Atlantic years, from 1967 to 1979, that the Queen would find her bold voice and emotional power. Whether singing her own songs or reimagining classic pop and R&B songs, the twists and turns of her voice moved as it grooved. She put the "R-E-S-P-E-C-T" into "Respect," turning a single by Otis Redding into a call to arms for the feminist and civil rights movements. With 1972's *Young, Gifted, and Black*, Lady Soul continued to show that there's pride in being just that.

The Queen would make a triumphant comeback in the 1980s, crossing over into dance pop with 1985's certified platinum *Who's Zoomin' Who* and collaborating over the decade with the Eurythmics, George Michael, and Whitney Houston. The following decade also had its shining moments. At the 1998 Grammy Awards, Aretha brought the house down with a last-minute performance of the aria "Nessum Dorma" after Luciano Pavarotti was too ill to perform. She'd hit the charts again that year with the Lauryn Hill song "A Rose Is Still a Rose."

The Queen of Soul remains one of the most honored artists in music history, with hits that span half a century. Throughout her reign, she changed music altogether, beginning with her pioneering sound in the 1960s, and showed that she could master the popular sounds of the decades that followed.

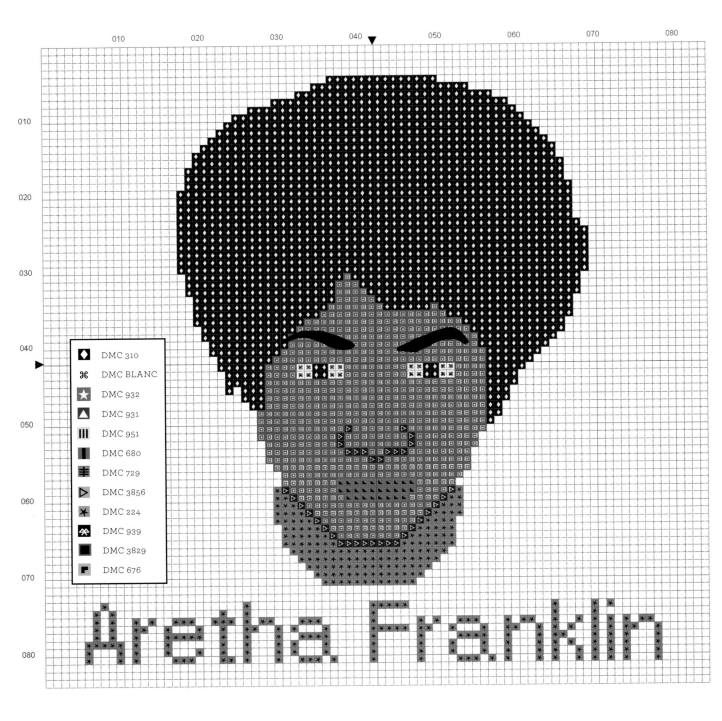

Aretha Franklin

CAROLE KING

◇◇◇◇◇ (1942–) ◇◇◇◇◇

SONGWRITER,
PRODIGY,
CREATOR

*C*arole King wrote the songs that still captivate the world. Outside of her own hits like "It's Too Late" and "So Far Away," she's written and cowritten timeless songs for the Shirelles, the Everly Brothers, Aretha Franklin, and James Taylor. Having composed over 400 songs, recorded by more than 1,000 artists, she remains one of the most successful songwriters of all time. Her work from the 1960s and 1970s is still in regular rotation on radio stations to this day.

A musical prodigy born and raised in New York City, King, born Carol Jean Klein, started playing piano at age 4 and writing songs at age 10. In high school, she started her first band, called the Cosines, and began selling her songs. At Queens College, she'd meet her songwriting partner of many years and first husband, Gerry Goffin. Together, the pair would write 1960's "Will You Still Love Me Tomorrow" for the Shirelles, the first hit by a girl group to reach number one on the *Billboard* Hot 100. King, who composed the melody to Goffin's lyrics, was only 17 years old.

King took on songwriting full time with Goffin, getting married and having kids along the way. The hits continued throughout the 1960s with "Take Good Care of My Baby" for Bobby Vee, "Up on the Roof" for the Drifters, and "One Fine Day" for the Chiffons. They even wrote a song for their babysitter, Little Eva, that hit number one, sparking a *brand-new dance* across America with 1962's "The Loco-Motion." The duo was there for the British Invasion, writing songs for the Beatles, the Animals, and Herman's Hermits. Before their marriage and partnership ended, they would have one of their biggest hits in 1967. After Aretha Franklin's producer yelled out of a car window that he needed a hit for the lesser-known Queen of Soul, the two got to work and wrote "(You Make Me Feel) Like A Natural Woman" in one night.

After her divorce from Goffin in 1968, King moved with her daughters to Laurel Canyon in Los Angeles and took on a new musical life among a like-minded crew of creators, but her stage fright prevented her from touring. Her solo 1971 album, *Tapestry*, became one of the most successful albums of its time, kicking off a new era in music for the singer-songwriter. The album led to four Grammy awards, the first for a woman at the time, and its songs resulted in number-one hits for King and James Taylor, for whom she wrote "You've Got a Friend."

In 2000, King recorded an updated version of "Where You Lead" from *Tapestry* for the theme music to *Gilmore Girls*, introducing a new generation to her legendary music. For her contributions to popular music and culture, she was honored in 2012 with the Library of Congress Gershwin Prize for Popular Song, the first woman to win the prize.

◆	DMC 310
⌘	DMC BLANC
★	DMC 932
▲	DMC 931
‖‖	DMC 951
▮	DMC 680
☰	DMC 729
▷	DMC 3856
✳	DMC 224
❊	DMC 939
■	DMC 3829
◪	DMC 676

JANIS JOPLIN

◇◇◇◇◇◇◇ (1943–1970) ◇◇◇◇◇◇◇

BLUES MAMA, FREE SPIRIT FRONTWOMAN

"She goes barefooted when she feels like it, wears Levis to class because they're more comfortable, and carries her autoharp with her everywhere she goes so that in case she gets the urge to break into song, it will be handy. Her name is Janis Joplin." So began a 1962 article from *The Daily Texan* by college student Pat Sharpe. Free-spirited Janis had always been an outsider—even long before her rockin' voice was shredding with the best of 'em.

As a kid, Janis was a loner. Raised in a conservative Texas oil town during the conformist 1950s, high school was hell. Her classmates bullied her for looking and being different, calling her a "freak" and a "pig." Blues music became an outlet during that period. As a teenager, she fell in love with artists like Bessie Smith and Odetta. Soon afterward, she ditched her college studies for her dreams. In 1963, she left home and began singing her own blues in coffeehouses and bars across Texas and then in San Francisco.

Janis's career as a folk/blues singer did not immediately take off, and her drinking and drug use held her back. She would often return to Texas after partying spells, trying to clean herself up and take on a more conventional life. In 1966, her friend told her that the psychedelic rock band Big Brother and the Holding Company were looking for a lead singer. Packing her bags again for San Francisco, she finally find her crowd. "All of a sudden, someone threw me in front of this rock and roll band," Janis said. "And I decided then and there that was it. I never wanted to do anything else."

Janis's powerful voice—much like her—was rough around the edges, packed with feeling, and had no bounds. The frontwoman of the rock band, a rarity at the time, blew the crowd away during a legendary performance at the 1967 Monterey Pop Festival. Their debut album, *Cheap Thrills*, came out shortly after and was a big success. Janis's blues-soaked voice, singing, "I'm going to show you baby, that a woman can be tough" on the hit "Piece of My Heart" quickly took on a life of its own. The blues mama left the band shortly afterward to pursue a solo career. Soon, she was cruising around San Francisco in her psychedelic Porsche like she owned the place—because she did.

Janis lived as hard as she rocked until her tragic death from a heroin overdose at 27. The posthumous *Pearl* was released in 1971. On the cover of the album, Janis looks like a hippie queen as she lounges in a Victorian love seat with feathers in her hair. Her powerful vocals are heard on every track except one, the instrumental "Buried Alive in the Blues," which she was supposed to record the day she died.

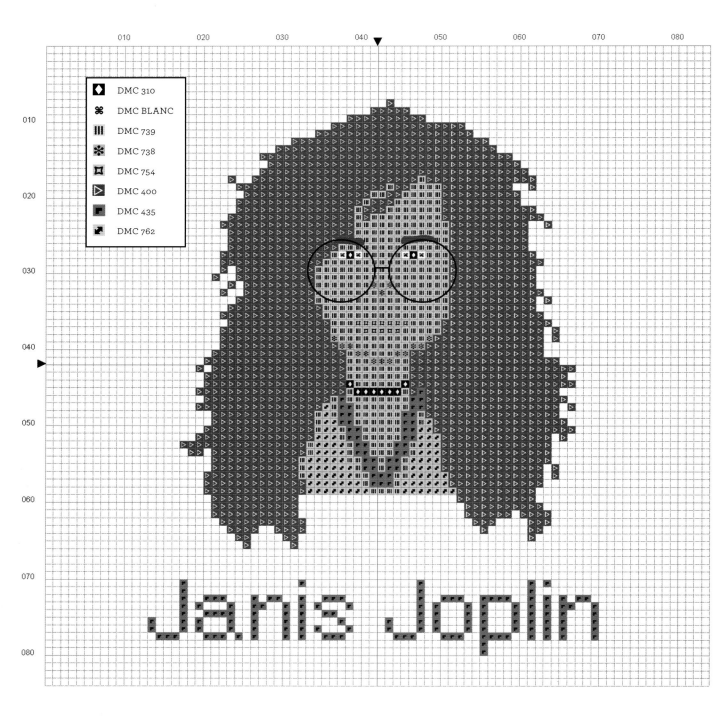

Janis Joplin

JONI MITCHELL

◇◇◇◇◇ (1943–) ◇◇◇◇◇

LYRICIST, INDEPENDENT THINKER, EXPERIMENTER

"**I**'m a very analytical person, a somewhat introspective person; that's the nature of the work I do," Joni Mitchell said in a 1979 *Rolling Stone* interview with Cameron Crowe. "But this is only one side of the coin, you know. I love to dance. I'm a rowdy. I'm a good-timer."

Joni, like the female experience captured in her songs, is complex. A self-described "painter derailed by circumstance," the singer-songwriter and inventive guitarist has always created on her own terms. While her male peers warned her not to reveal too much in her lyrics, she knew better than to listen. Her honest portrayal of love, lust, life, and loss gave her music emotional roots that extended beyond her own experience.

Born Roberta Joan Anderson and raised on the Canadian prairie of Saskatchewan, she contracted polio at age nine. Her long hospital stay transformed her from a talented athlete into a sensitive, creative soul. As a teenager, Joni taught herself ukulele to entertain her friends at bonfire parties, and later on, in art school, she learned how to play guitar with the help of a Pete Seeger songbook. With her left hand damaged by polio, Joni had to get creative with her tunings and develop a new way of playing chords. She took her distinctive way of playing into the coffeehouses of Toronto, leaving college in 1964.

There, Joni met American folksinger, Chuck Mitchell, and married him at 21. The two moved to Detroit and toured the United States before she left him for a solo career in 1967, which took her up and down the East Coast and out to the hills of Laurel Canyon. Famous artists like Judy Collins and Dave Van Ronk covered songs she wrote in her early 20s, like "Chelsea Morning" and "Both Sides Now," and found their own success. Meanwhile, Joni was kicking off her reign of the folk kingdom with her 1968 debut album, *Song to a Seagull*.

With her deep, thoughtful lyrics; unique guitar style; and voice soaring to new heights, Joni quickly cemented her legacy with the groundbreaking albums that followed: *Clouds* (1969), *Ladies of the Canyon* (1970), *Blue* (1971), *For the Roses* (1972), *Court and Spark* (1974), *The Hissing of Summer Lawns* (1975), and *Hejira* (1976). Her genius as a lyricist came not just from her ability to describe a range of human emotions, but to evoke them. Fiercely independent and uncompromising, she also stayed true to her art as it changed over the years, experimenting with elements of jazz, classical, and electronic music.

With a pensive look on her face and a cigarette in her mouth, Joni showed the world what it meant to be female and free.

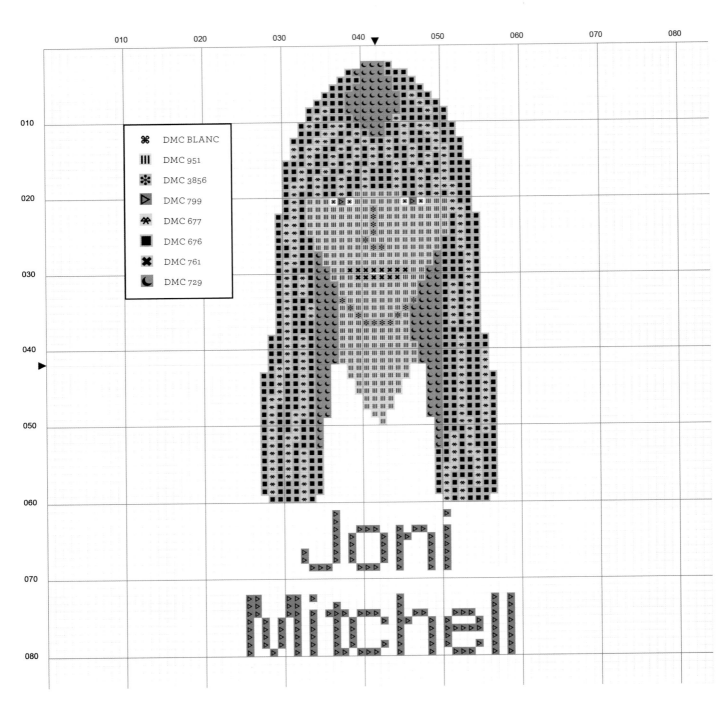

✿	DMC BLANC
▮▮▮	DMC 951
✳	DMC 3856
▷	DMC 799
✤	DMC 677
■	DMC 676
✖	DMC 761
☾	DMC 729

DIANA ROSS

◇◇◇◇◇ (1944–) ◇◇◇◇◇

DISCO DIVA,
ACTRESS,
MOTOWN STAR

The Supreme Queen and disco diva ruled with glamor and grace. With her big hair and glittery gowns, Diana Ross shaped the Motown sound of the 1960s with the Supremes before coming into her own with hits like "Ain't No Mountain High Enough" and "Upside Down." With number-one singles as a solo artist, part of a duet, a member of a trio, and part of an ensemble from the 1960s to the 1980s, her drive was as endless as the love she so often sang about.

Before becoming Diana to the world, she was "Diane" to her family in the Detroit projects—the result of an "e" being marked as an "a" on her birth certificate. By age 15, Diana was singing in the Primettes, a sister act of the all-male vocal group the Primes. In 1960, Diana's childhood friend Smokey Robinson landed the group an audition at Motown Records in exchange for their guitarist, Marv Tarplin. While Diana's voice stopped Berry Gordy, head of Motown, in his tracks, he told the four Primettes to come back after high school. The girls continued to hang around Hitsville USA, providing handclaps and backing vocals wherever needed.

Their persistence paid off. After changing their name to the Supremes, they were signed to a record deal in 1962. By 1964, the quartet became a trio, Diana took over lead vocals, and "Where Did Our Love Go" landed at number one on the *Billboard* charts. The four singles that followed— "Baby Love," "Come See about Me," "Stop! In the Name of Love," and "Back in My Arms Again"— all made it to number one, setting a record for consecutive chart toppers. Supremes-mania was in full force as Motown's "sweethearts" won over audiences with their polished look and pop soul sound. By the end of the 1960s, they were the most popular girl group in the world. "Someday We'll Be Together" was the group's 12th and final number one before Diana made her exit.

Diana remained a mainstay on the radio airwaves in the decades that followed. As a solo artist, she had six number-one singles, including the 1975 disco classic "Love Hangover," the 1980 anthem "I'm Coming Out," and the 1981 ballad "Endless Love" with Lionel Ritchie. She also starred on the big screen as Billie Holiday in *Lady Sings the Blues* (1973) and Dorothy in *The Wiz* (1978), cohosted Johnny Carson's *Tonight Show*, and joined with other artists for USA for Africa's "We Are the World" in 1985. As the music world changed, Diana always stayed in fashion. Her music even found its way into the 1990s as the Notorious B.I.G. and Janet Jackson sampled her famous tracks.

◆	DMC 310
⌘	DMC BLANC
◣	DMC 3859
≡	DMC 758
⬚	DMC 3778
▷	DMC 3371
◐	DMC 946
▦	DMC 900

DEBBIE HARRY

◇◇◇◇◇ (1945–) ◇◇◇◇◇

BOMBSHELL,
ADVENTURER,
LEADER

Blondie Is a Group! read the band's 1979 button campaign, in pink letters on a black background. As the new wave group emerged from the New York punk underground in the late '70s, the peroxide blonde on vocals soon became synonymous with the band itself. As its frontwoman, Debbie Harry demanded attention. While many were arrested by her blonde bombshell looks, it's her energy and work as a vocalist and songwriter that really turned the music world upside down.

With Blondie, Harry helped pioneer a distinctive sound that effortlessly grooved from one genre to the next. That unique ability can be seen in the disco-influenced "Heart of Glass," the cover of the rocksteady "The Tide is High" and "Rapture," which made her the first rapper to top the *Billboard* charts. Harry was more than just the face of Blondie. She was its cool attitude and sound.

Raised a Jersey girl, Harry moved to New York City in the late 1960s. Before Blondie, she worked as a secretary, a go-go dancer, a Playboy Bunny, and a waitress at the legendary Max's Kansas City, where the group would later become regulars. She got involved in the New York underground art and punk scenes in the early '70s, sharing vocals with two other women in a group called the Stilettos. When Chris Stein, a guitarist and Harry's future boyfriend, saw her onstage, he was entranced. By 1974, the two were playing in Blondie opposite the Ramones and the Patti Smith Group at CBGB's. The two had come up with the band's name after someone yelled from a car at Harry.

The band released their debut album, *Blondie*, in 1976. While the band's mainstream success would come later, with 1978's *Parallel Lines*, it was clear from early on that the band and its lead singer were bringing something fresh to the music scene. While some of their biggest hits, including "Heart of Glass" and "Call Me," were influenced by disco, they also were undoubtedly Blondie. The band continued to be adventurous in the albums that followed, bringing an eclectic group of sounds from the past and present to the forefront.

While Blondie, the band, would split up in 1982, the influence that Debbie Harry had as its frontwoman on the world is undeniable. While she looked like any other Hollywood blonde, her real appeal came from her intelligent lyrics and ability to take on different personas both onstage as Blondie and later in film.

DMC 310
DMC BLANC
DMC 948
DMC 744
DMC 321
DMC 407"

DOLLY PARTON

(1946–)

INSTRUMENTALIST,
QUEEN OF COUNTRY,
GLAMOR ICON

It's hard to believe that Dolly Parton is real, and the country superstar would be the first to joke that she's not. Onstage, she's often hollers, "There ain't much real about me but my heart," and, "It pays a lot of money to look this cheap!"

Beneath the wigs and the one-liners is a brilliant songwriter and musician who's built a rhinestone empire out of dirt. Dolly has written over 3,000 songs, plays everything from the guitar to the autoharp, and is the only artist to have top-20 hits across six consecutive decades from the 1960s to the 2010s. She's also been nominated for a Grammy, an Oscar, an Emmy, and a Tony. Few can match her level of glam or natural charm, and to do it all while growing up with so little is truly incredible. But she wasn't crowned the Queen of Country for nothin'.

Dolly was the fourth of 12 kids, all raised in a one-room cabin in the Tennessee mountains. Growing up hearing Appalachian folk music and spirituals in church, she started singing at 6 and playing guitar at 7. By 1959, the 13-year-old was releasing her debut single "Puppy Love" and being introduced by Johnny Cash at the Grand Ole Opry. She moved to Nashville after graduating from high school to pursue a career in country music. Having written a number of songs for other artists while working on her own material, she soon became a regular on *The Porter Wagoner Show*.

While Dolly's first solo hit would come with "Dumb Blonde" in 1967, one of the few songs she didn't write, she still proved that she was anything but. Dolly protected the publishing rights to all the songs she did write, ensuring that she'd maintain control of her work and be paid fairly for it. With her thoughtful lyrics and distinctive voice, she got her first number one on the country charts with "Joshua" in 1971 and one of her biggest with the haunting "Jolene" two years later. In 1974, she wrote "I Will Always Love You" after parting professional ways with her former duet partner. The song would hit number one twice in its lifetime, once on the country charts for Dolly and again for Whitney Houston in 1992.

The Queen of Country was just scratching the surface with her pretty fingernails. In 1977, Dolly crossed over into pop with the release of *Here You Come Again*, the title track of which became her first pop hit. The 1980 song "9 to 5" was a success on both the country and pop charts, quickly becoming a working woman's anthem. Starring in the film by the same title, Dolly played a secretary who teams up with female coworkers to get back at their sexist boss, a plot line that feels as relevant today as it did in 1980.

Dolly is a living legend in every sense of the phrase. One of the most successful country artists ever, she's always stayed true to her roots, living by her own words from 1971's "Coat of Many Colors" that "One is only poor, only if they choose to be."

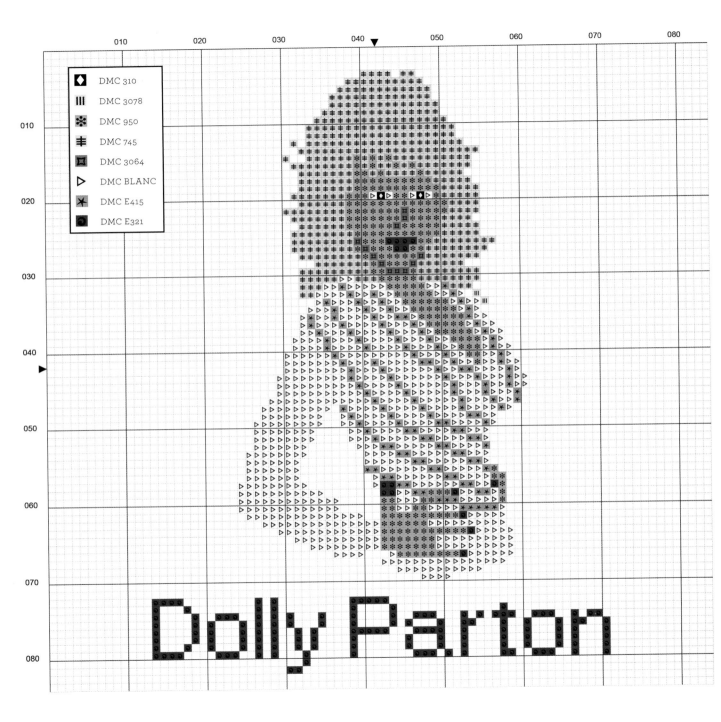

	DMC 310
	DMC 3078
	DMC 950
	DMC 745
	DMC 3064
	DMC BLANC
	DMC E415
	DMC E321

Dolly Parton

PATTI SMITH

◇◇◇◇◇ (1946–) ◇◇◇◇◇

POET,
VISUAL ARTIST,
ACTIVIST

The poet laureate of punk found her words before her wild voice, which breathed a new life into rock 'n' roll. In 1968, the 21-year-old was an aspiring artist working in a New York bookstore when she first saw the Doors play. As she recalled in her memoir *Just Kids*, while the rock star Jim Morrison had the entire audience in a trance, her reaction was different—she thought without reservation, "I could do that."

Raised in Philadelphia and South Jersey by working-class parents, Patti always had an artistic vision for herself. While she was frequently sick growing up, the writings of Arthur Rimbaud and the records of Bob Dylan kept her company in her bedroom. The thin, gangly teen also loved rock and jazz music. An underage Patti was even kicked out of a Philly nightclub for sneaking into a John Coltrane show. After high school, she took a miserable job at a tricycle factory, which she would later sing about in her first single, the 1974 poem-turned-punk song "Piss Factory." By the end of the song, Patti's ambitions eventually win out as she chants over banging piano keys, "I'm gonna be somebody, I'm gonna get on that train, go to New York City, I'm gonna be so bad I'm gonna be a big star and I will never return."

Patti left her rough-and-tumble life in Jersey for a new one up the turnpike. In New York, she wrote poetry, plays, and reviews of rock shows for *Creem* and *Rolling Stone*. She also found her crowd in fellow artsy misfits like photographer Robert Mapplethorpe, who convinced Patti to turn her poems into lyrics, and guitarist and rock writer Lenny Kaye. Lenny put his rock guitar to Patti's words, which she'd growl and scream defiantly onstage.

The Patti Smith Group became regulars at CBGB's and were the first from the emerging New York punk scene to land a record deal. Patti's debut album *Horses* (1975) kicked off a new era in musical experimentation with its dark, expressive lyrics and unfiltered energy playing out over three simple chords. Patti's iconic look, captured by her friend Robert on the album cover, was as unconventional as her sound. Straggly-haired and in a man's shirt, she is unapologetically herself and does not care what anyone thinks of her. The fresh attitude that she took toward her art and herself jolted both the literary and punk worlds into a new era.

"I seriously worried that I was seeing the decline of rock and roll," Patti once said about her early days. "My design was to shake things up, to motivate people and bring a different type of work ethic back to rock and roll."

Patti
Smith

STEVIE NICKS

◇◇◇◇◇ (1948–) ◇◇◇◇◇

DREAMER,
LEAD VOCALIST,
BOHEMIAN

Some call her sister of the moon. Some say illusions are her game. With her big, deep voice and dreamy lyrics, the gypsy queen of rock 'n' roll possesses a strange magic. In the 1970s, her tales of love and heartbreak transformed Fleetwood Mac into one of the greatest rock bands of all time. Her songs have since empowered generations of broken hearts to *pick up the pieces and go home.*

Before the layers of velvet and lace, kid Stevie was singing her first harmonies at Arizona gin mills with her country-singing grandfather. The Nicks family moved throughout Stevie's teenage years before landing in Palo Alto, California. After getting a guitar for her 16th birthday, she wrote her first song about life after heartbreak. In 1966, she met Lindsey Buckingham at a party during her senior year in high school. While he was strumming "California Dreamin'" on his guitar, Stevie joined in on the harmonies. Two years later, they were playing in the psychedelic rock band Fritz together. With Stevie on lead vocals, they opened for Jimi Hendrix and Janis Joplin, one of her influences as a frontwoman, before breaking up in 1971.

Stevie and Lindsey fell in love, moved to Los Angeles, and continued to collaborate in the years that followed. They released one album as Buckingham Nicks in 1973. Then Lindsey was asked to join Fleetwood Mac, a British blues band that had moved to California with soft rock dreams, and he insisted that Stevie come, too. She wrote and sang on two of the group's earliest hits—"Rhiannon" and "Landslide"—from their 1975 self-titled album.

Following a period of emotional upheaval in which bandmates Christine and John McVie divorced, Stevie and Lindsey split, and Mick Fleetwood's wife cheated on him, the group wrote through their own heartbreak and recovery on 1977's *Rumours*. The album spent 31 weeks at number one and remains one of the best albums of all time. Many of the record's big hits were penned by the women in the band, including the group's first number-one hit, the Stevie song "Dreams."

Free-spirited Stevie also found success in her solo career outside of Fleetwood Mac. Her debut album, 1981's *Bella Donna*, made it to the top of the charts with hits like "Edge of Seventeen," which she wrote during a period of grief, and "Stop Draggin' My Heart Around," a duet with Tom Petty. As a musician and a woman who's lived, she would release more hits on her own and with Fleetwood Mac over the next two decades.

As she sings in "Silver Springs," a B-side from *Rumours* that was released on 1997's *The Dance*, "Time cast a spell on you, but you won't forget me."

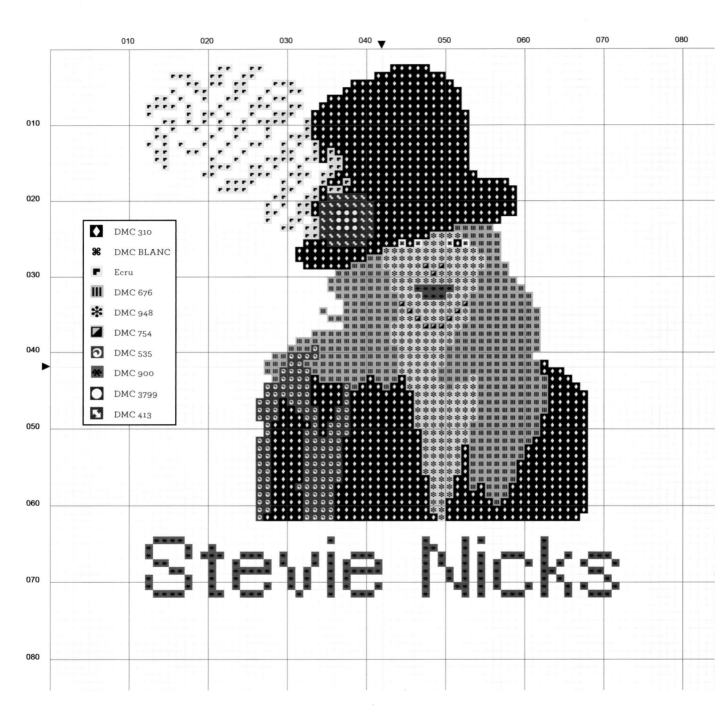

◆	DMC 310
✿	DMC BLANC
◤	Ecru
⫴	DMC 676
✳	DMC 948
◩	DMC 754
◓	DMC 535
✾	DMC 900
●	DMC 3799
◩	DMC 413

MADONNA

◇◇◇◇◇ (1958–) ◇◇◇◇◇

SUPERSTAR,
MAVERICK,
QUEEN OF POP

"**How could I have been anything else but** what I am, having been named Madonna. I would either have ended up a nun or this," the music superstar famously once said.

The patron saint of pop music and culture pushed social boundaries throughout her career, changing the music scene for women in the face of criticism from both feminists and the Vatican. Throughout her career, Madonna showed the world that there was no shame in being sexy, intelligent, and comfortable expressing yourself.

Before rolling around onstage in a provocative wedding dress, Madonna Louise Ciccone was one of six kids raised by strict Catholic parents in Michigan. Growing up, she was a straight-A student, cheerleader, and skilled dancer whose talent landed her a college scholarship. Madonna dropped everything after two years to pursue a dancing career in New York in 1977. As she recalled, "It was the first time I'd ever taken a plane, the first time I'd ever gotten a taxicab. I came here with $35 in my pocket. It was the bravest thing I'd ever done."

During her first year in New York, Madonna was held up at gunpoint, robbed multiple times, and assaulted on the way home from a dress rehearsal. Those traumatic experiences only provided fuel for her fire, as she tried to make it. By 1982, she would go on a world tour as a backup singer; dance, play drums, and sing in the rock band the Breakfast Club; and cut her first solo club hit with "Everybody." Madonna moved from the club to the radio after releasing her eponymous debut album in 1983, which contained the international top-10 hits "Holiday," "Lucky Star," and "Borderline."

Throughout the 1980s, Madonna kept the dance floors packed with the decade-defining albums that followed, including *Like a Virgin* (1985), *True Blue* (1986), *You Can Dance* (1987), and *Like a Prayer* (1989). MTV broadcast the pop sensation into living rooms across America, triggering a cultural shift. Women across the globe started dressing in her image, attitudes about sex and sexuality changed, and the male-dominated world of pop got a much-needed makeover.

Throughout her career, Madonna constantly reinvented herself, trading in her crucifix necklace for a cone-shaped bra, exploring a life on the big screen with roles in *Desperately Seeking Susan* and *Evita*, and changing her popular sound with the times. Still, she never lost her Madonna-ness.

Crowned Woman of the Year by *Billboard* in 2016, she gave a special shout-out to those who doubted her or shunned her work, letting them know, "Your resistance made me stronger, made me push harder, made me the fighter that I am today. It made me the woman that I am today."

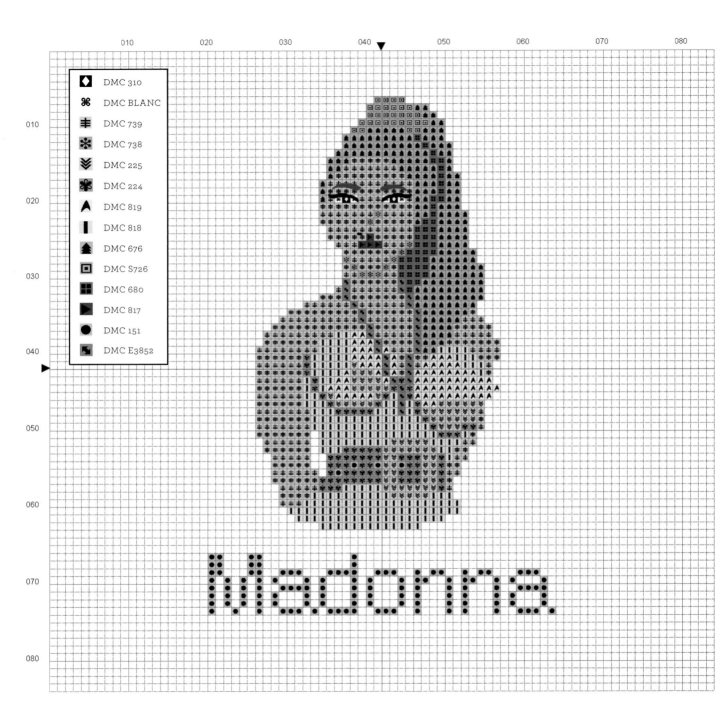

JOAN JETT

◇◇◇◇◇ (1958–) ◇◇◇◇◇

FEMINIST ICON,
ROCKER,
REBEL

Joan Jett is rock 'n' roll stripped down to its basic elements. Equal parts hard and punk rock, with a touch of glam, the shaggy-haired guitarist has been playing loud and fast since she was 15. From founding the all-girl band the Runaways to hitting it big with the Blackhearts, the guitarist, songwriter, and record producer helped break up the old classic rock boys' club. And she did it all with the same defiant sneer that she wears to this day.

Born outside of Philadelphia in 1958, Jett fell in love with rock 'n' roll early in life. Getting her first guitar for Christmas at 13, she famously quit after being pushed to play folk music. It wouldn't be until her family moved to southern California that she'd receive a proper education in power chords at Rodney Bigenheimer's English Disco. The teen frequented the LA nightclub, where she listened to her favorites, including David Bowie and Suzi Quatro. It was also at Rodney's that Jett first ran into Hollywood record producer, Kim Fowley, and expressed interest in starting an all-female band.

A few calls and rehearsals later, the Runaways were exploding onto the scene with a "Hello world! I'm your wild girl. I'm your ch-ch-ch-ch-ch-cherry bomb!" Composed by Jett, the 1976 single remains a classic. The teen queens of noise continued to rock in the years that followed, releasing four studio albums, selling out shows in Japan, and touring with the Ramones. Still, the girls had trouble selling albums in the United States, dismissed by rock fans as a gimmick.

While the Runaways broke up in 1978, Jett was far from done. She produced the only album by the LA band the Germs (*GI*), one of the first hard-core punk records, in 1979. She also went to London to work on solo material, including a cover of "I Love Rock 'n' Roll" by the British group the Arrows. Returning to LA, she got to work recording a self-titled solo album with producer Kenny Laguna. After the album was rejected by 23 major labels, the two decided to start their own outfit. The album, which they released themselves in 1980, was rereleased a year later as *Bad Reputation* after its iconic title track.

Jett continued to find success by following her heart over the haters. Hiring the Blackhearts to back her, they hit it big in 1982 with *I Love Rock 'n' Roll*, which included the famous barroom anthem as the title song. That song has sold over 10 million copies to date, remaining in regular radio rotation to this day. While Jett would continue to churn out hits and play to large crowds throughout the '80s, it's her cool attitude and love of rock that's truly admirable. By breaking social norms to do what she wanted to do, she showed a future generation of riot grrrls and rock 'n' rollers that anything's possible.

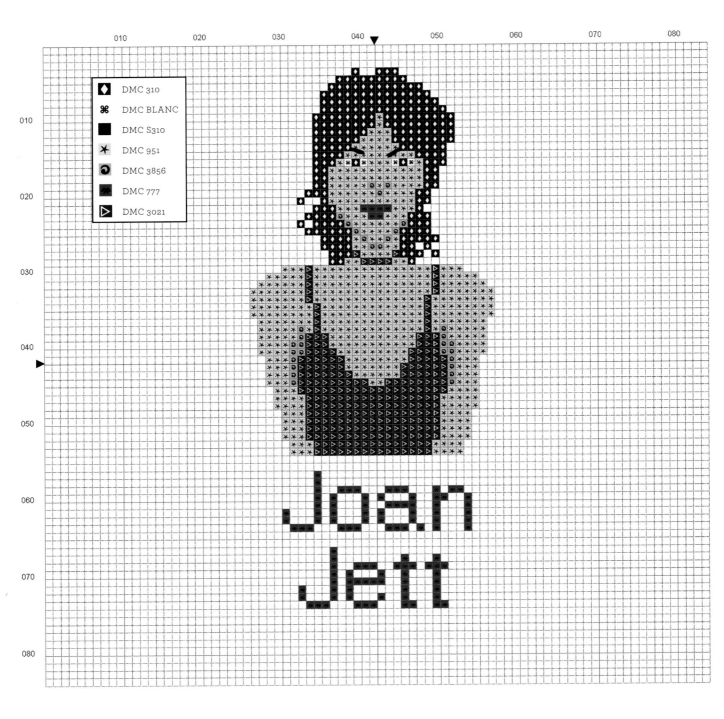

DMC 310
DMC BLANC
DMC S310
DMC 951
DMC 3856
DMC 777
DMC 3021

Joan
Jett

WHITNEY HOUSTON

◇◇◇◇◇◇ ◈ (1963–2012) ◈ ◇◇◇◇◇◇

R&B DIVA,
MODEL,
CHAMELEON

Whitney's voice makes you feel. From the perfect pop chorus of "How Will I Know" to *the note* in "I Will Always Love You," her range could move audiences to either the dance floor or to tears within moments. The pop and R&B diva had a unique ability to take a song captive, effortlessly rebuilding it into her own. Whether it was a country classic, a '70s soul ballad, or "The Star-Spangled Banner," she left audiences frozen, feeling like they were experiencing greatness for the first time.

Born into a family of female musical royalty, Whitney had good genes. Her mother, Cissy, was an R&B and gospel singer who did backup vocals for Elvis Presley, Otis Redding, Jimi Hendrix, and Aretha Franklin. Her cousin, Dionne Warwick, topped both the pop and R&B charts in the '60s and '70s, paving the way for the crossover sound that Whitney embraced in the decades that followed. When an 11-year-old Whitney made her singing debut in church, it was obvious that she, too, had talent. Soon afterward, a teenage Whitney was singing in local nightclubs with her mama and doing backup vocals for Chaka Khan—whose "I'm Every Woman" she would later turn into a dance hit.

When the head of Arista Records, Clive Davis, saw a young Whitney performing at a New York nightclub, he immediately signed her to a record deal. At 23, she released her debut album, *Whitney Houston*, which included three number-one hit songs, among them "Saving All My Love for You," landing her the first of many Grammy awards. The hit parade continued with her follow-up album, 1987's *Whitney*. "I Wanna Dance with Somebody (Who Loves Me)" was the first of four hits from the album that made it to the top of the *Billboard* charts, making Whitney the first artist in music history with seven consecutive number-one hits and the only female artist with four number ones on the same album.

Whitney's talent had no bounds in the years that followed, as she starred opposite Kevin Costner in 1992's *The Bodyguard*. Her legendary cover of "I Will Always Love You," a 1974 country hit for Dolly Parton, appeared on the film's soundtrack. With its flawless climactic build, her rendition spent a record-breaking 14 weeks at number one and remains one of the top-selling singles of all time. Yet while Whitney had perfect control of every note, her personal life was more chaotic. The voice of her generation struggled with the demands of fame, love, and drug use until her death in 2012.

Still, it's her voice that will continue to resonate over the drama, the strength that she exudes in the "Greatest Love of All" when declaring, "No matter what you take from me you can't take away my dignity."

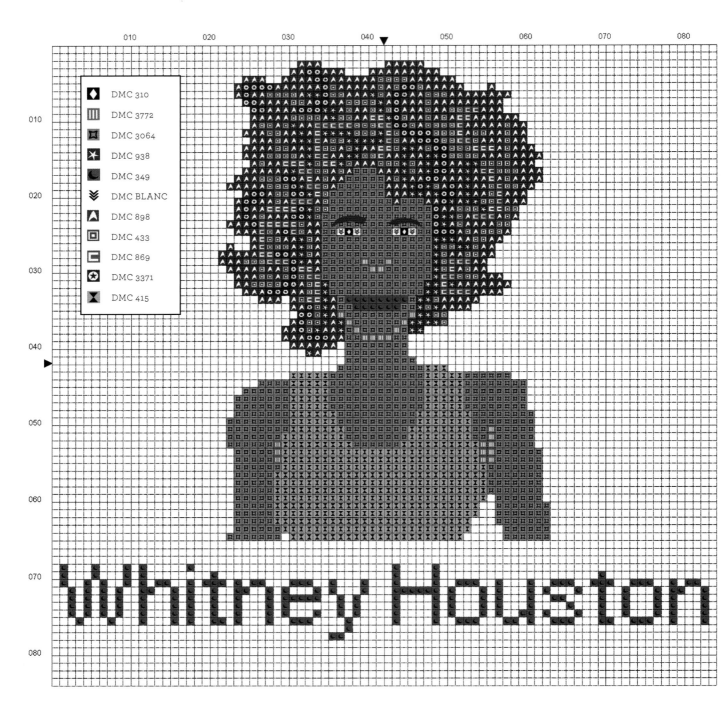

	DMC 310
	DMC 3772
	DMC 3064
	DMC 938
	DMC 349
	DMC BLANC
	DMC 898
	DMC 433
	DMC 869
	DMC 3371
	DMC 415

KATHLEEN HANNA

(1968–)

FEMINIST ACTIVIST, PUNK PIONEER, WRITER

"I never thought of myself as a musician, rather a feminist performance artist who played someone in a band," Kathleen Hanna said in a recent interview with *The Guardian*. The lead singer of the 1990s punk band Bikini Kill helped put the *grrrl* in Riot Grrrl. Her music and writing empowered women to get into punk, freely express themselves, and speak out against injustice.

Born in Portland, Oregon, Kathleen first learned about feminism from her mom, a homemaker and frequent reader of *Ms.* Young Kathleen would cut out pictures from the magazine and make posters that said things like "Girls can do everything," as she noted in a 2000 interview with *BUST Magazine*. At age nine, her political vision became clear when her mom took her to a Solidarity Day rally in Washington, D.C., of which she said, "It was the first time I had ever been in a big crowd of women yelling, and it really made me want to do it forever."

Her activist passion only grew deeper. At Evergreen State College in the late 1980s, she put together a photo exhibit with a classmate that focused on sexism. When the exhibit was taken down by college officials within days, that prompted Kathleen and her friends to open their own feminist art gallery, where they also played in a band. At the same time, Kathleen threw herself into spoken-word poetry. When she told Kathy Acker that she got into it because she had a lot to say, the feminist writer responded, "Then why are you doing spoken word—no one goes to spoken-word shows! You should get in a band."

In Olympia, Washington, she met Tobi Vail, a punk zine writer about "angry grrls" who used to play in the Go Team. They joined up with guitarist Billy Karren and bassist Kathi Wilcox to form Bikini Kill. Politically aware in their words and powerful in their performances, songs like "Rebel Girl" and "The Anti-Pleasure Dissertation" became underground anthems, lighting a fire for the Riot Grrrl movement and the rise of third wave feminism. The band faced sexism onstage at the same time as they fought it in their lyrics, dealing with verbal and physical abuse as they played. The Bikini Kill zine, which began in 1991, called for making the male-dominated scene they played in a more inclusive space while providing helpful mosh pit safety tips.

Shortly before Bikini Kill broke up in 1998, Kathleen got to work on a lo-fi solo project as Julie Ruin before playing with the electronica outfit Le Tigre into the 2000s. While she began experimenting with new sounds, her inner riot raged on as her words were set to new beats.

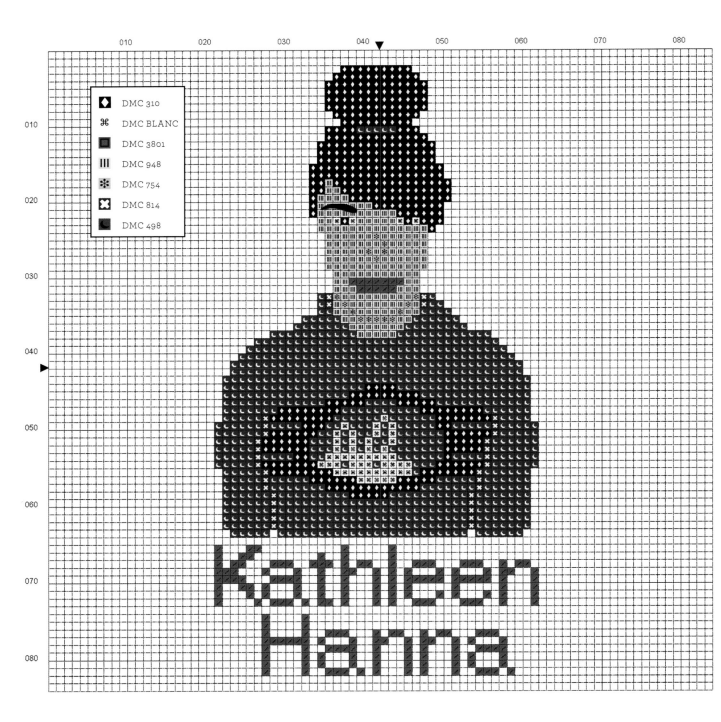

SELENA

◇◇◇◇◇◇◇ (1971–1995) ◇◇◇◇◇◇◇

QUEEN OF TEJANO, ENTERTAINER, DESIGNER

The "Queen of Tejano" brought people together as she sang and shimmied her way from a small town in Texas to the top of the *Billboard* charts. Selena gave male-dominated Tejano music a female voice, tore down cultural walls by bringing a local genre of Spanish-sung music to the masses, and showed that being "Latina" and "American" weren't mutually exclusive. While the crossover pop star would leave the world too soon at 23, her legacy lives on in the continuing *bidi bidi bom bom* of her fans' hearts.

Selena Quintanilla was born in Lake Jackson, Texas to working-class Mexican-American parents. Her father, Abraham, noticed her perfect pitch and timing when she was just six years old. He immediately got to work putting together a family band. Abraham opened the Mexican restaurant Papagayos, and the kids became the nightly entertainment. While a recession would lead the restaurant to close and their family to leave town in the early 1980s, the band stayed together, playing gigs at quinceañeras, fairs, and local gatherings across Texas as Selena's popularity grew.

Selena wanted to sing songs in English, which she spoke, but her father encouraged her to embrace her heritage and record Tejano or Tex-Mex music, which mixed elements of polka, jazz, and country. With his guidance, Selena learned to sing in Spanish phonetically. Over time, she became fluent, allowing her to better connect with the Latino community. Still, venues weren't interested in booking a Tejano band with a female singing lead, and promoters warned that she'd never make it. The smiley teen and her powerful voice proved them all wrong, winning the Tejano Music Award for Female Vocalist of the Year in 1987. And it was all up from there.

Selena's 1990 album of ballads and cumbias, *Ven Conmingo*, became the first Tejano album to go gold, selling over 500,000 copies. Her next album blended the traditional with the sounds of R&B, rock, disco, and pop. With "Como la Flor," 1992's *Entre a Mi Mundo* climbed to the top of the *Billboard* Regional Mexican Albums chart. Selena became the first female Tejano artist to win a Grammy for best Mexican/American album for *Live!* in 1994. That same year, she released *Amor Prohibido*, which had four number-one singles and remains one of the best-selling Latin albums of all time. While she was touring for the album, fans from all backgrounds came out in record-breaking numbers to see her shake her way from disco classics to Mexican cumbias.

The music came to a sudden halt when Selena was fatally shot by the founder of her fan club in 1995. The album *Dreaming of You* was released posthumously and became the first by a Latin artist to debut at number one on the *Billboard* 200. Mixing English-language ballads like "I Could Fall in Love" with her Latin hits, the album crossed musical and cultural boundaries, much as Selena herself had.

◆	DMC 310
✳	DMC BLANC
Ω	DMC 3856
▶	DMC 347
✳	DMC 436
◣	DMC 3031
◯	DMC 3371
✖	DMC E168
◨	DMC E3852

MISSY ELLIOTT

◇◇◇◇◇ (1971–) ◇◇◇◇◇

RAPPER,
BUSINESSWOMAN,
CHOREOGRAPHER

"Me I'm supa fly, supa dupa fly, supa dupa fly," Missy Elliott repeats while pop-locking in a black inflated trash bag and gold sunglasses that fit like a crown. In the iconic video for her debut single "The Rain," she made her rule of the hip-hop kingdom boldly, unquestionably clear. She was more than just another rapper with a hit on the *Billboard* charts. Missy "Misdemeanor" was a producer, songwriter, arranger, choreographer, businesswoman, and innovator whose work shaped hip-hop culture in the 1990s and beyond.

The future had been on Missy's mind since she was a kid growing up in Portsmouth, Virginia. A bright only child, she skipped two grades early in school and dreamed of becoming an entertainer. Still, her home life was turbulent. Growing up in poverty, she was abused by an older cousin and her father beat her mother on a regular basis. To cope, she often wrote letters to the musicians she admired, like Janet Jackson and Diana Ross, hoping that they would one day come to her rescue.

In the late 1980s, Missy formed the all-female R&B group Fayze, which would later be renamed Sista after signing a record deal in 1991. Shortly afterward, Missy moved to New York to work within the Swing Mob hip-hop collective. The first hit she wrote and rapped on was young Raven-Symoné's "That's What Girls Are Made Of." When the directors cast a thin, light-skinned model to lip-sync her rap, the fuller-figured, dark-skinned Missy was crushed. She threw herself into songwriting and producing.

Missy and her neighborhood friend Tim "Timbaland" Mosley, created many of familiar radio sounds of 1990s radio. They produced and wrote Aaliyah's *One in a Million* in 1996 as well as tracks by SWV, Total, and Destiny's Child. Missy worked as a featured vocalist on *One in a Million* and for a remix of one of her songs by Sean "Puffy" Combs, who wanted to sign her as a solo artist to Bad Boy Records. Choosing instead to continue writing and producing for herself and others, Missy started her own label, The Goldmind Inc., to ensure that she would remain the sole architect of her sound and image.

Her 1997 album, *Supa Dupa Fly*, was the highest-charting debut by a female rapper to date. It was also the first major release in which a woman rapped, wrote, and produced every song. As a solo artist, Missy would continue to work it, from "Get Ur Freak On" to "Lose Control." In her career to date, she has also written, produced, remixed, and rapped on tracks for a number of other artists, including Whitney Houston, Madonna, and even her childhood hero, Janet Jackson.

Missy made the hip-hop world a more interesting place. While running around in outer space fighting robots with Lil' Kim and Da Brat in the video for "Sock It 2 Me," she showed black girls everywhere that the universe had potential.

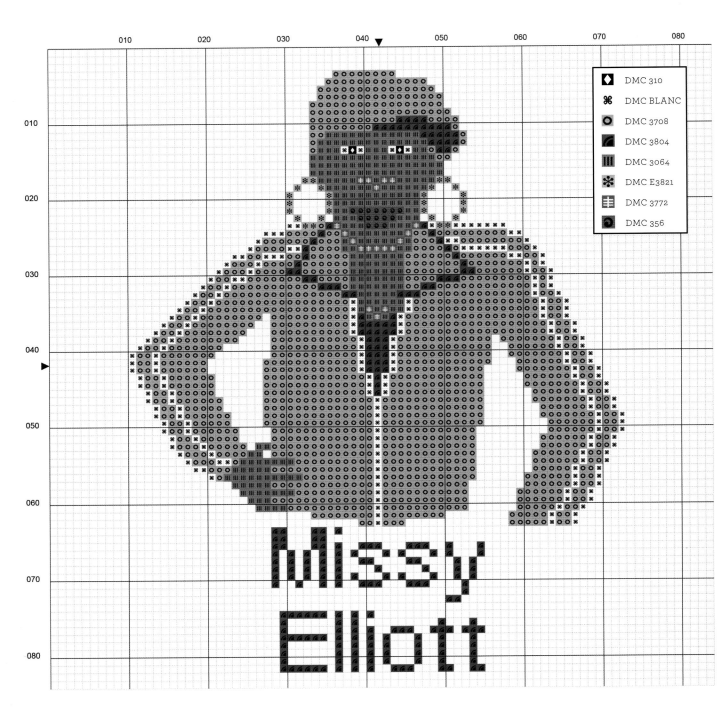

LAURYN HILL

◇◇◇◇◇ (1975–) ◇◇◇◇◇

SONGWRITER,
RECORD PRODUCER,
ACTRESS

Lauryn Hill has always preached what she's practiced. As one-third of the Fugees and the force behind 1998's *The Miseducation of Lauryn Hill*, L-Boogie wove her personal rhymes into life lessons about sexual politics, prejudice, and social responsibility. Her unique blend of soul, reggae, R&B, and rap went just as deep as her lyrics, revolutionizing hip-hop music altogether. Ms. Lauryn taught girls of the 1990s that they deserved to have it all, including respect, which she reminds us is *just a minimum* in "Doo Wop (That Thing)."

Lauryn grew up in South Orange, New Jersey, surrounded by piles of old soul records. Her mother was a teacher who played piano and her father was a computer consultant and singer. Lauryn began making her own music in high school after meeting classmate Pras Michel. The teens dreamed up a hip-hop group that could sing and rap in different languages. Soon, they were performing as a trio with Pras's older cousin, Wyclef Jean, as the Tranzlator Crew. Multitalented, Lauryn sang lead vocals before she taught herself how to rap and began writing her own rhymes. As book-smart as her lyrics were street-smart, she attended Columbia University before leaving college to focus on her music career.

The Tranzlator Crew later became the Fugees and landed a record deal. Soon, Lauryn was singing "Ooh la la . . ." as their 1996 album *The Score* took the hip-hop world to new heights. With its sharp lyrics and magical blend of the fresh with the familiar, the record peaked at number one on both the *Billboard* 200 and Top R&B/Hip-Hop Albums chart. The group's biggest hit came with their bold rendition of Roberta Flack's 1973 hit "Killing Me Softly with His Song," which *Spin* called "an instant classic, pumped out of every passing car from coast to coast, with Lauryn Hill's timeless voice never losing its poignant kick."

With the world still super-high off the Fu-gee-la, the singer, songwriter, rapper, and producer left both the group and her turbulent relationship with Wyclef behind in 1997. While pregnant with her first son by Rohan Marley, son of Bob Marley, she threw herself into working on what would become the 1998 masterpiece, *The Miseducation of Lauryn Hill*. Drawing on her love of old-school sounds and personal experiences, the album flows like conversation. Lauryn effortlessly shifts from hard-hitting raps about how fame changes everything on "The Lost Ones" to the criticism she faced as a female artist for wanting to be a mother in "To Zion."

Her words, told from an honest female perspective, were just as cutting as the raw beats that accompanied them.

AMY
WINEHOUSE

◇◇◇◇◇◇◇ (1983–2011) ◇◇◇◇◇◇◇

VOCALIST,
ORIGINAL,
OLD SOUL

Behind the towering beehive, Cleopatra makeup, and tattoos was a raw genius that had no match. The hard-living Amy Winehouse was as real as they come. The lyrics she wrote were brutally honest. "Rehab" and "You Know I'm No Good" read like pages from her diary. And the way her brassy voice took hold of each word, as if her heart were being ripped out of her chest, was just as real. While her tragic fall from fame would be well-documented, the soul singer's edginess came more from her truth than the tabloid stories. As Steve Kandell wrote in a 2007 story for *Spin*, "Music's most authentic punk is a 23-year-old white Jewish girl from the London suburbs who sings like a lost Supreme."

Amy was born an old soul, raised by a working-class family in Southgate. She grew up loving jazz and listening to Ella Fitzgerald, Sarah Vaughan, and Dinah Washington. With her early appreciation for the classics also came a love for modern R&B and rap. As a 10-year-old, Amy formed a hip-hop duo with her best friend, called Sweet 'n' Sour, in which Amy naturally brought the sour. Still, her musical talent wouldn't be realized until she became a featured vocalist in the National Youth Jazz Orchestra. And when her friend sent the 16-year-old's demo tape to a record label, the rest was history.

Her debut album, *Frank*, came out in 2003. The jazz-influenced record was critically acclaimed in the UK, both for Amy's powerful, sultry voice as well her painfully frank lyrics. From calling out her older man as a "lady boy" in "Stronger Than Me" to singing through her self-destructive ways in the twisted "Amy Amy Amy," it's clear that the 19-year-old had already *lived*. *Back To Black*, released in 2006, traded in jazz for the sounds of '60s girl groups and Motown, but the same deep feelings were there.

The album led to international success and five Grammys, tying the record at the time for most wins by a female in one night, but the drama that surrounded her actual life would soon take over. While Amy would have another hit with "Valerie," the downward spiral that led to her death from alcohol poisoning at 27 would be a tragic one.

To quote music writer Ann Powers in a piece following Amy's death, "Those of us who took pleasure in the fruits of Amy Winehouse's inner turmoil now have to acknowledge its ultimate end. As we contemplate this, we can also revel in what was most entrancing about her music: its brashness and utterly engaging power, the upfront expression of a woman who was loud without apology. Her big notes still live."

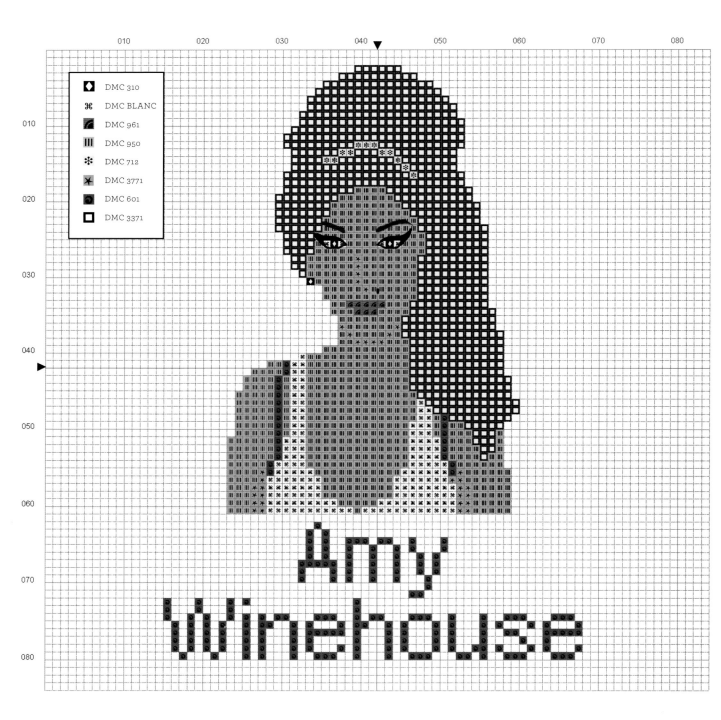

◆	DMC 310
⌘	DMC BLANC
◪	DMC 961
Ⅲ	DMC 950
✳	DMC 712
✶	DMC 3771
◖	DMC 601
☐	DMC 3371

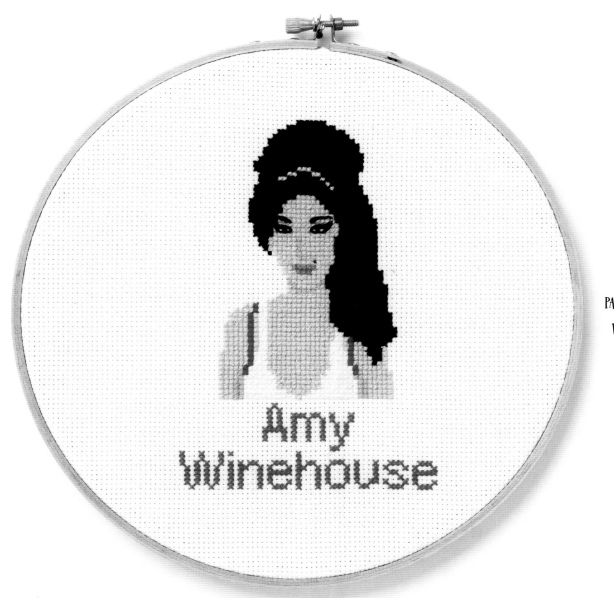

Amy
Winehouse

LADY GAGA

(1986–)

MOTHER MONSTER, PHILANTHROPIST, UNCONVENTIONAL ICON

Lady Gaga rescued the pop world from boredom. With a growing band of "little monsters" behind her, Mother Monster transformed the late aughts with her over-the-top sound and otherworldly looks. The experimental pop superstar demanded the world's attention with a "ro mah ro-mah-mah." She kept the spotlight on her as she danced from an underground club to a jazz joint to a local dive, showing her fans that there's beauty in being both different and yourself.

Gaga was born Stefani Joanne Angelina Germanotta and raised Catholic on New York's Upper West Side. Naturally talented, she started playing piano at age 4 and was performing in nightclubs by the time she was a teenager. Granted early admission to New York University's Tisch School of the Arts at 17, she left during her sophomore year to focus on her music career. Over the next few years, Gaga hustled, playing in clubs on the Lower East Side, writing songs for Britney Spears and the Pussycat Dolls, and performing in the burlesque act, called "Lady Gaga and the Starlight Revue."

Signed and dropped by Def Jam records and then signed by Interscope, she faced resistance early in her career for not fitting into the pop mold. As she noted in a 2009 interview with *The Independent*, "They would say, 'This is too racy, too dance-oriented, too underground. It's not marketable.' And I would say, 'My name is Lady Gaga, I've been on the music scene for years, and I'm telling you, this is what's next.'"

Gaga was right. Her debut album, 2008's *The Fame*, won a Grammy for Best Dance/Electronica Album and became an international success with hits like "Just Dance" and "Poker Face," the best-selling single of 2009. *The Fame Monster* EP followed, with pop hits like "Bad Romance," "Alejandro," and "Telephone," featuring Beyoncé. And 2011's *Born This Way* was Gaga's biggest epic yet, with its anthems about self-acceptance and sexuality. The five-foot-two pop powerhouse was unstoppable, her elaborate performances and outrageous outfits as etched into the public consciousness as her catchy choruses.

In the years that followed, she proved her versatility. Gaga released a hit album of jazz duets with Tony Bennett, won a Golden Globe for acting on *American Horror Story*, had her 2016 album *Joanne* top the country charts, and jumped off the roof of a Super Bowl stadium in her 2017 halftime performance. The fame monster also used her platform to bring important issues to the forefront, including LGBTQ rights, youth empowerment and bullying, and sexual assault, writing "Til It Happens to You" with Diane Warren.

With her empowering music and "Don't be a drag, be a queen" mantra, Lady Gaga made music both more interesting and more accepting.

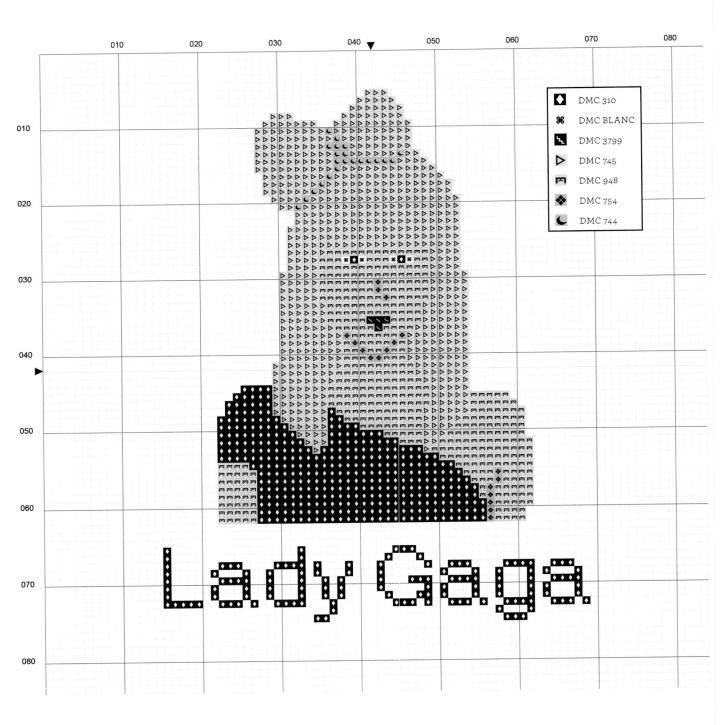

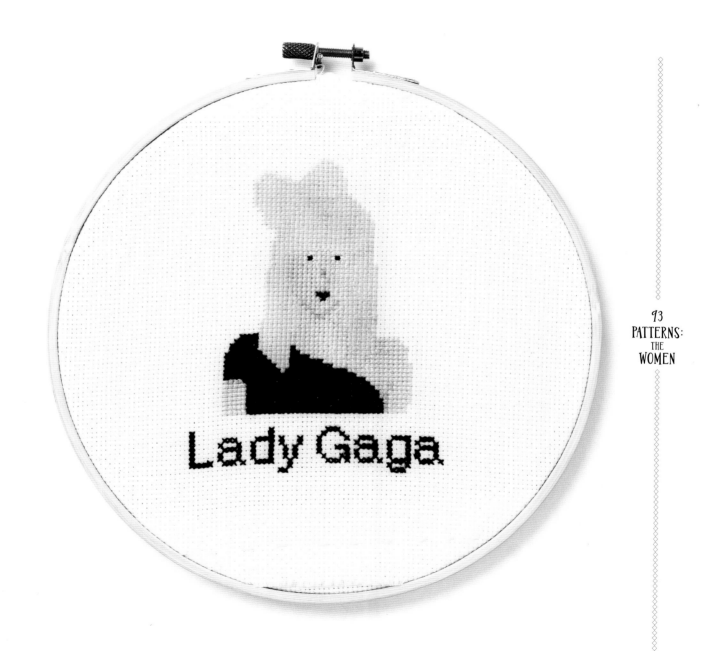

Lady Gaga

PATTERNS:
THE SONGS

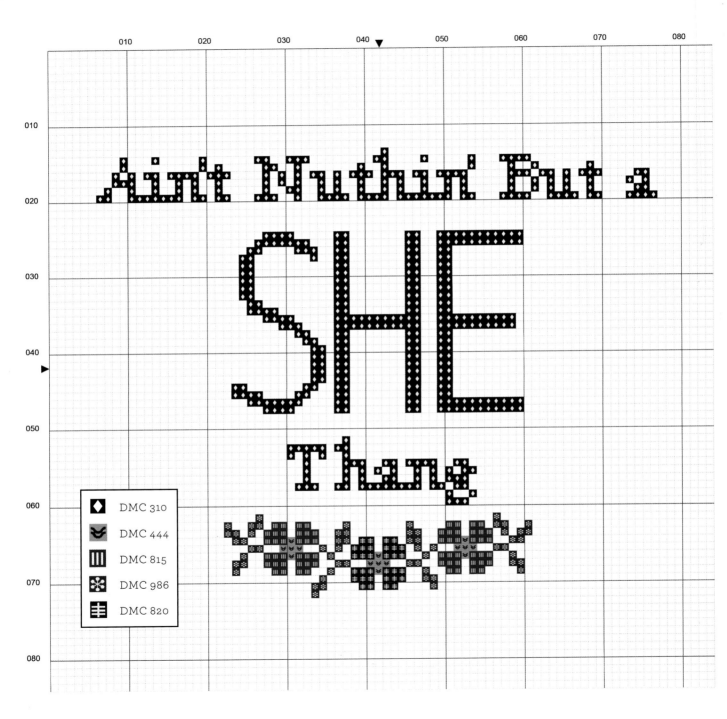

Aint Nuthin' But a SHE Thang

	DMC 310
	DMC 444
	DMC 815
	DMC 986
	DMC 820

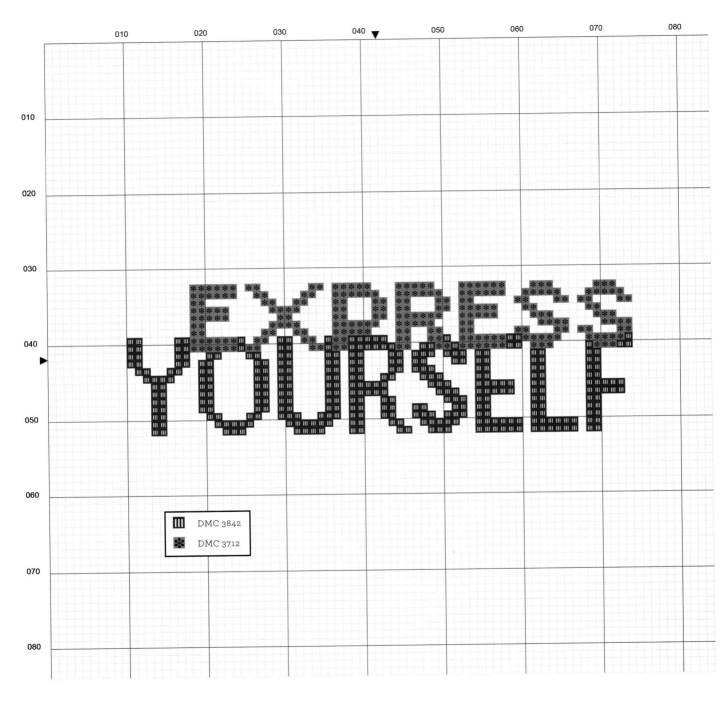

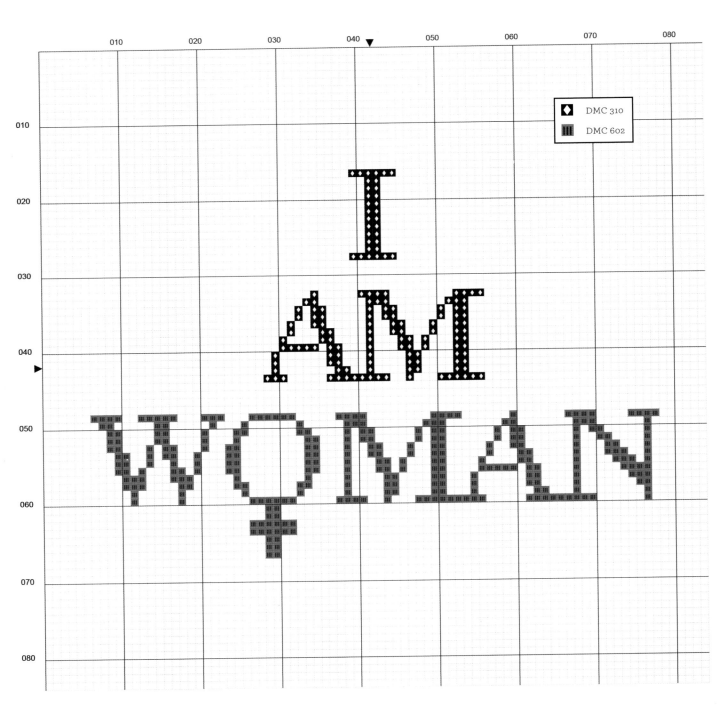

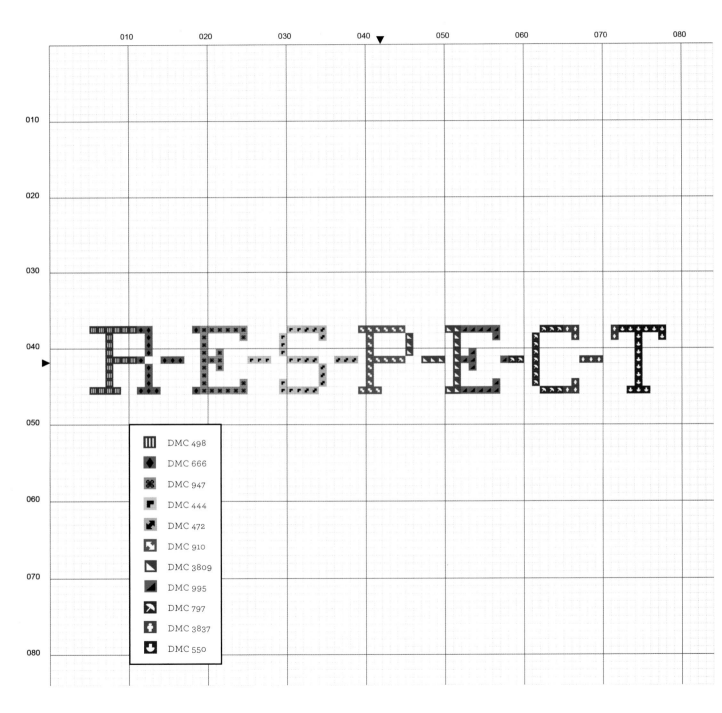

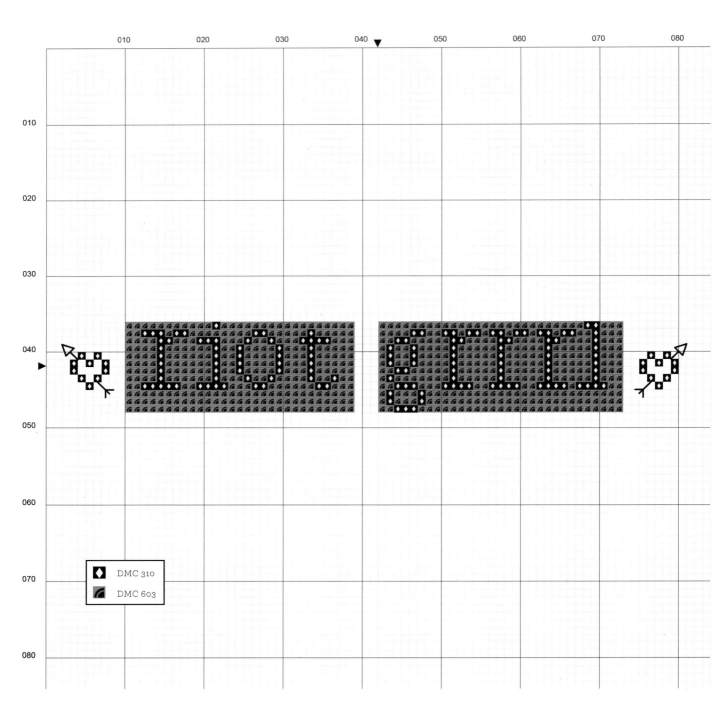

DMC 310

DMC 603

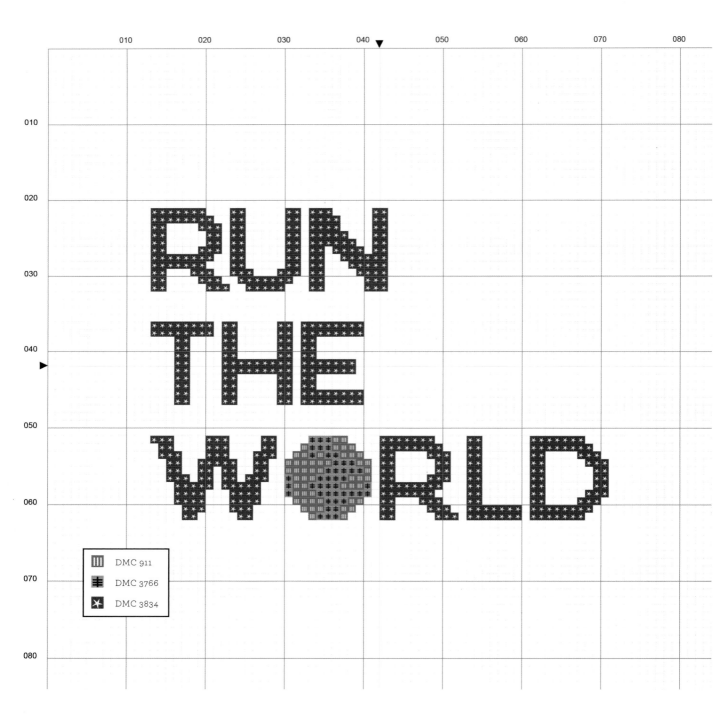

DMC 911
DMC 3766
DMC 3834

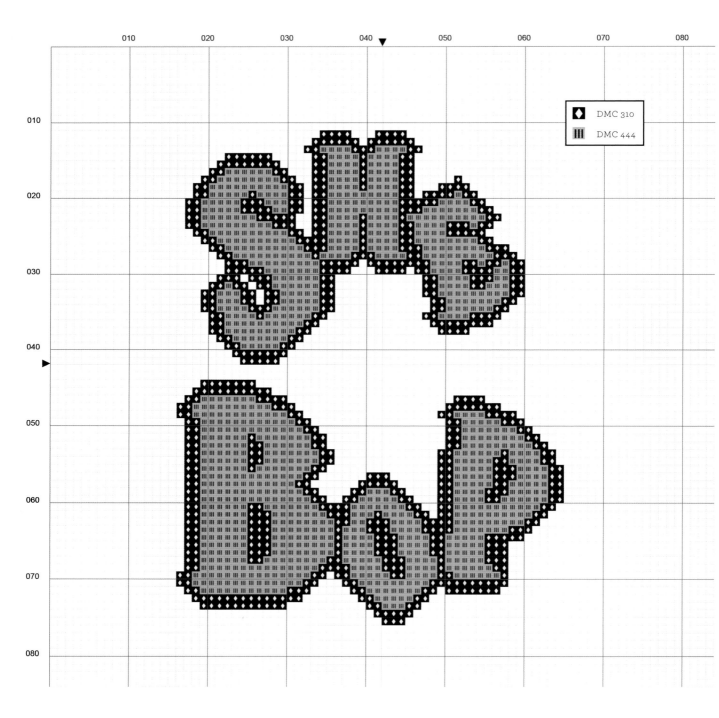

ACKNOWLEDGMENTS

You'd think that after six months of creating content, writing a paragraph about the people I know best would be easy. But just like every pattern tells a story, it would take infinite paragraphs to explain exactly how instrumental you all were to this process. Thank you to my friends and family for not letting me lose sight of myself while I lost myself in the stories of the great women in this book. Stitch on, rockstars.

—ANNA FLEISS

A supergroup of rockin' women made this book possible. Thank you to Shannon Connors Fabricant, editor supreme, for your encouragement, patience, and shared love of Fleetwood Mac. Thank you to my amazing co-author, Anna Fleiss, for these creative stitches, and to designer Amanda Richmond for putting together another beautiful book that tells the important stories of women worth celebrating.

And thank you to those that have been boppin' next to me all along—my Dad for keeping the Diana Ross cassettes close when I was a kid, Kathryn for standing next to me at shows when not onstage rockin' yourself (Long Hots forever), and Josh for making me mixtapes and being my date to the Dolly show. I love you all.

—LAUREN MANCUSO

INDEX